It Came Upon A Midnight Clear

It came up-on the mid-night clear, That glo-rious song of old,

Especially for

From

Date

# The Carols of Christmas

## A Celebration of 40 Beloved Songs of the Season

David McLaughlan

BARBOUR
PUBLISHING

ISBN 978-1-60260-651-7

Cover illustration by Tommy Hunt. Interior scores by David Silberman.

Published by Barbour Publishing, Inc., P.O. Box 719, Uhrichsville, Ohio 44683
www.barbourbooks.com

*Our mission is to publish and distribute inspirational products offering exceptional value and biblical encouragement to the masses.*

ecpa  Member of the
Evangelical Christian
Publishers Association

Printed in China.

# Contents

Section 1:

Carols of Peace

# God Rest Ye Merry, Gentlemen

God rest ye merry, gentlemen, let noth-ing you dis-may.

God rest ye merry, gentlemen;
Let nothing you dismay.
Remember Christ, our Savior,
Was born on Christmas day,
To save us all from Satan's pow'r
When we were gone astray.
O tidings of comfort and joy,
comfort and joy!
O tidings of comfort and joy!

# God and the Watchmen

Surprisingly, there are no "merry gentlemen" in this Christmas carol—unless we count the fellows doing the singing! All being well, the gentlemen referred to would have been in nightshirts and nightcaps and sound asleep. The comma between *merry* and *gentlemen* suggests it's their rest that should be merry, not the gentlemen!

The authors of this song of redemption are unknown, but tradition has it they were watchmen, paid extra by the local burghers to guard the town over the Christmas period. Their job usually would have involved patrolling the nighttime streets with a lamp. They would announce the time on the hour, following that with a reassuring "And all's well!" At some point though, perhaps overcome by the Christmas spirit, they seem to have started singing!

Reminding their cozy patrons that they were saved through Christ, the watchmen also encouraged those listening to love each other in Christian brotherhood. All hearing their song should entrust their night's rest to God, and the knowledge of Satan's inevitable defeat should be enough to make that rest a merry one.

Surprisingly in such a happy song, Satan is mentioned twice, but the presence of his name does nothing to lessen the overwhelming "tidings of comfort and joy!"

The tune may have been brought to the English West Country by French merchants, but the lyrics were born on the streets of an unknown English town in the fifteenth century. The publication, in 1833, of *Christmas Carols Ancient and Modern* brought them to a wider audience.

In taking the news of Christ's birth out into the frosty street with a joyful song, those unknown believers may well have been the world's first Christmas carolers. If the watchmen could have foreseen how popular caroling would become, they probably would have been very merry gentlemen indeed!

*Sing unto him, sing psalms unto him,*
*talk ye of all his wondrous works.*
1 Chronicles 16:9

# A Lullaby for the World

Some things in this world—melodies, concepts, prayers—touch the human soul so deeply it would almost be a shame to ascribe them earthly authorship. "Away in a Manger," the first carol many children ever learn, encompasses our feeling of Christmas so completely that it might have been a gift to the world rather than something teased from a mind and scratched out in pen and ink.

Fittingly, no one knows who came up with the first two verses, although the image of reforming clergyman Martin Luther singing it over his children's cradles has proven remarkably durable despite there being no proof he wrote the carol. It does, however, fit beautifully with Luther's belief that all comfort and rest are to be found in God.

The third verse, beginning with "Be near me," appears slightly later and, despite having various claimants for authorship, ultimately remains as mysterious as the rest.

The carol (or lullaby, sometimes called "Cradle Song") first surfaced in America rather than Luther's Germany with the publication, in 1885, of a Lutheran Sunday school book. It popped up again, two years later, in *Dainty Songs for Little Lads and Lasses* and has been a much-loved part of the festive celebrations ever since, especially with children.

The idea that the Lord was once a child who needed cared for, just like them, appeals to the little ones. But it's an appeal that doesn't seem to wane as those children grow older. When adult carolers sing, "Bless all the dear children in Thy tender care, and fit us for heaven to live with Thee there," you just know the children they are singing about still live in their hearts.

"Away in a Manger" is a lullaby to the Lord—and to the world.

*And she brought forth her firstborn son,*
*and wrapped him in swaddling clothes, and laid him in a manger;*
*because there was no room for them in the inn.*

Luke 2:7

Away in a Manger

A - way in a   man - ger,   no   crib   for   a   bed,

Away in a manger,
No crib for a bed,
The little Lord Jesus
Laid down His sweet head.
The stars in the sky
Looked down where He lay,
The little Lord Jesus
Asleep on the hay.

## Heard the Bells on Christmas Day

I heard the bells on Christ-mas day Their old fa-mil-iar car-ols

I heard the bells on Christmas day
Their old familiar carols play,
And wild and sweet the words repeat
Of peace on earth, goodwill to men.
I thought how, as the day had come,
The belfries of all Christendom
Had rolled along the unbroken song
Of peace on earth, goodwill to men.

# The Bells Still Ring

Underlying the joy and wonder of the Nativity is the never-to-be-forgotten fact that Jesus came to this world because we *needed* Him. Left to its own devices, humanity tends to take the downward path. This fact must have been all too painfully obvious while men fought kinsmen and countrymen in the American Civil War.

Months away from the end of the conflict, having lost his wife and having received news of his son's injury in battle, Henry Wadsworth Longfellow put pen to paper and wrote the poem "Christmas Bells." Given the dreadful situation in which he found himself, it would have been understandable if his work became an ode to hopelessness.

Longfellow *did* write about humankind's dire condition: "And in despair I bowed my head. 'There is no peace on earth,' I said, 'for hate is strong and mocks the song of peace on earth, goodwill to men.'"

Yet, despite what the poet and his country were going through, the poem is one of hope and deliverance. "God is not dead," he wrote, "nor doth He sleep; the wrong shall fail, the right prevail."

Twelve years after peace was restored, John Baptiste Calkin, English composer and music teacher, rearranged "Christmas Bells." He left out the more overt references to the war, making the message more universal, and set it to the tune of "Waltham." So a poem born at the height of a bloody conflict made the transition to Christmas carol.

"I Heard the Bells on Christmas Day" is a message, sent to us through the faithful heart of a great poet, that in times of national crisis or times of personal need, the Lord (whatever anyone else may say) is there for each one of us.

Because we needed Him, He came. And the chiming bells remind us—He is still here!

*For God hath not appointed us to wrath,*
*but to obtain salvation by our Lord Jesus Christ.*
1 Thessalonians 5:9

# The Angels Still Sing

All times have their trials, and for the past two thousand years, all times have the answer to those trials.

In Edmund Sears's time the most pressing trials involved the "Forty-niner" gold rush, industrialization, and buildup to civil war. In Jesus' time it was the dominion of the Roman sword. And today? Well...

This gentle minister wrote a beautiful poem pointing out that no matter what our woes, the solution is right there for each of us. Ten years later Richard Storrs Willis was so inspired by the poem, he put it to music, creating one of the earliest American Christmas carols.

Sears never mentions the Nativity, but his image of mighty angels bending low reminds us that they were there for a purpose—to announce the birth of Christ.

In telling us the angels still hover above, singing "that glorious song of old," Sears makes it plain that Christ is still here, or the angels would have gone home long ago!

The problem is not God, he says; the problem is us. The world has deafened itself by the sounds of conflict until it no longer seems to hear the beautiful music of salvation.

Come Christmastime, when the frantic shopping is done, when the family has been fed and the gifts opened, when the hubbub dies down, wouldn't that be the perfect time to listen awhile? Then take that moment of communion forward and find a space for it in each day of the new year.

The angels still sing. We just need to lay aside our earthly cares and still our earthly noises long enough to hear them. No, we need to do more than that!

As Sears points out, those angels won't be satisfied until they hear us singing "that glorious song of old" right back at them!

*Also I say unto you, Whosoever shall confess me before men,*
*him shall the Son of man also confess before the angels of God.*
Luke 12:8

# It Came upon the Midnight Clear

It came up-on the mid-night clear, That glo-rious song of old,

It came upon the midnight clear,
That glorious song of old,
From angels bending near the earth
To touch their harps of gold.
"Peace on the earth, goodwill to men,
From heaven's all-gracious King."
The world in solemn stillness lay
To hear the angels sing.

O Little Town of Bethlehem

O lit-tle town of Beth-le-hem, how still we see thee lie

O little town of Bethlehem,
How still we see thee lie!
Above thy deep and dreamless sleep
The silent stars go by.
Yet in thy dark streets shineth
The everlasting Light;
The hopes and fears of all the years
Are met in thee tonight.

# The Unchanging Promise

Bethlehem today doesn't bear much resemblance to the Bethlehem of biblical times. It seems like everything changes—but some truths are eternal.

In 1865 Rector Phillips Brooks of Philadelphia was given a wonderful view of one such truth. Journeying on horseback from Jerusalem to Bethlehem, Brooks stopped for the night in the hills above his destination.

Even in 1865 Bethlehem would have been quite different from Jesus' time, but Brooks was struck by the fact that this sleeping town was where the Lord came to earth. That fact would never change, and neither would the message He brought.

Assisting in a Christmas service in the "little town," Brooks seemed to hear voices he knew well proclaiming the wonder of that holy birth.

He recorded his emotions in a poem that he showed to church organist Lewis Redner. Legend has it that the tune came to Redner on Christmas Eve and the Sunday school choir sang it for the first time the very next day.

As Brooks sat in the silence of the hills, that first Nativity must not have seemed so long ago, because the consequences of it were still very present in his mind, just as they are still present in the world today.

As he points out in his beautiful carol, "Where meek souls will receive him still, the dear Christ enters in."

Even in an age of security fences and army patrols, wherever children pray, wherever misery cries out, wherever charity watches and "faith holds wide the door," Jesus will be there.

Bethlehem, like the rest of the world, has changed and will continue to change—but, as Brooks realized while watching that sleeping town, wherever a willing heart calls Christ to come in and stay, sins will be cast out and, no matter how many years have passed since the first one, it will be Christmas once more.

*And thou Bethlehem, in the land of Juda,*
*art not the least among the princes of Juda:*
*for out of thee shall come a Governor,*
*that shall rule my people Israel.*
Matthew 2:6

# What Marks Us Out

Christina Georgina Rossetti was the daughter of an Italian political refugee. The family settled in London early in the nineteenth century and made a lasting impact in the artistic community. Christina's brother, Dante, went on to help found a new painting style with the Pre-Raphaelite Brotherhood. Meanwhile, she acquired her own fame as a poet—one of her most famous works being the poem that went on to become the hymn "In the Bleak Midwinter."

The interests of brother and sister combined when Dante asked Christina to model for his painting "The Girlhood of Mary Virgin," in which she, as Mary, is shown embroidering with her mother while a baby angel awaits the time to tell her of her destiny as the Lord's mother.

God became Christina's abiding passion. She turned down at least two marriage proposals because the suitors did not share her faith.

Away from the creative world, Christina proved her faith a real thing through her long-term commitment to and hands-on work in a refuge for "fallen" women. That love in practice at the cost of time, comfort, and perhaps even the respect of some of her peers, is reflected in "Love Came Down at Christmas."

Originally called "Christmastide," the poem was printed for the first time in 1885 in *Time Flies: A Reading Diary*. Later it was combined with a traditional Irish melody called "Garton," to become the Christmas song sung today.

"Love Came Down at Christmas" slips delicately and in a few, simple words straight to the heart of Jesus' mission on earth—that humankind should love God and each other.

God became human for us—and in her hymn Christina Rossetti asks how best we might repay that gift, how we might show the Lord, and each other, that we are His. We need a token, she decided. Something to identify us. And that "sacred sign" could only be love, "to God and all men."

*By this shall all men know that ye are my disciples,*
*if ye have love one to another.*
John 13:35

# Love Came Down at Christmas

Love came down at Christ-mas, Love all love-ly, love di-vine;

Love came down at Christmas,
Love all lovely, Love divine;
Love was born at Christmas,
Star and angels gave the sign.
Worship we the Godhead,
Love incarnate, Love divine;
Worship we our Jesus:
But wherewith for sacred sign?

## Silent Night

Si - lent night, ho - ly night, All is calm, all is brig

Silent night! holy night!
All is calm, all is bright
Round yon virgin mother and Child.
Holy Infant, so tender and mild,
Sleep in heavenly peace;
Sleep in heavenly peace.

# The Christmas Truce Carol

The romantic version of the "Silent Night" story has an Austrian priest at his wits' end when the church organ breaks down on Christmas Eve. With the prospect of a silent night ahead, he and the organist come up with a new hymn that can be sung without accompaniment. The result, "Silent Night," goes on to become one of the most popular Christmas carols of all time.

The real story (according to Silent Night Museum in Salzburg, Austria) is grittier but possibly more inspirational.

Joseph Mohr was born illegitimately in a time when illegitimacy halted any possibility of social progress. Fortunately, his singing voice caught the ear of the cathedral choirmaster, and he was encouraged into the priesthood.

Working as an assistant priest, he helped translate hymns from Latin to German, to the delight of parishioners and the fury of the church establishment. Mohr's liberal priest was replaced by a hard-liner.

Resenting Mohr's popularity, the new priest attempted to blacken his reputation by bringing up his illegitimate beginnings. The battle of wills culminated on Christmas Eve 1818 when the church organ mysteriously died. Mice were blamed, but another likely suspect was Mohr's friend, organist Franz Gruber. He put music to lyrics Mohr had written two years before, and "Silent Night" had its first public performance. It was sung in German with a guitar accompaniment, something that normally never would have been allowed.

The carol's popularity in both German and English made it the one song both armies could sing in unison from their trenches during the Christmas truce of 1914.

Joseph Mohr died in 1863. He left this world as poor as he came into it, having given everything he had for the sake of the poor. Not only did the life of this relatively unknown priest benefit his parishioners, but it glorified his Lord and gave the whole world a beautiful reminder of the night the world fell silent lest it wake a newborn baby.

*And again, when he bringeth in the firstbegotten into the world, he saith,*
*And let all the angels of God worship him.*
**Hebrews 1:6**

# A Lullaby to the World

"Still, Still, Still" is one of the most relaxing Christmas carols. Lacking the traditional verse and chorus format, it repeats the first word of each verse three times in a gently hypnotic fashion. The melody rises and falls like soft breathing, so it's no great wonder that "Still, Still, Still" was often used as a lullaby to soothe children to sleep.

As with many traditional songs, its origins are lost in time—and it is even difficult to find a definitive version of the lyrics. It was first sung in Austrian villages prior to 1819, and it spread by word of mouth with mothers and fathers singing it to their children as they remembered it, adapting it here and there.

By 1819 the lyrics had become attached to "The Salzburg Melody," and written copies were circulated. Variations in the words still persisted, but the differences really made no difference. The themes of rest, comfort, and reassurance shine through regardless of which version is sung. The song, seemingly sung by a mother to her child, might just as easily have been crooned by a loving God to a fretful humankind.

The snow is falling on Christmas Eve (the carol tells us), and nothing need disturb our sleep. God's angels are attentive and His love is all-encompassing. He is sending His Son to be born for our sake, and when we wake in the morning, everything will be different. Our problems will have a solution. Adam's fall will be redeemed.

So sleep and don't worry. God has it all in hand.

A beautiful and comforting promise—one we are reminded of every Christmas.

Overly simplistic, perhaps? Well, of course, it *isn't* as easy as all that; we still have our very important part to play. We have to allow ourselves to be loved.

*So the Levites stilled all the people, saying,*
*Hold your peace, for the day is holy;*
*neither be ye grieved.*
Nehemiah 8:11

# Still, Still, Still

An-gels, from the realms of glo-ry, Wing your flight o'er all the earth;

Still, still, still
One can hear the falling snow.
For all is hushed,
The world is sleeping,
Holy Star its vigil keeping.
Still, still, still,
One can hear the falling snow.

Section 2:

Carols of Wonder

# Home to Glory

James Montgomery, author of "Angels, from the Realms of Glory," was a gentle man, but he didn't shirk from criticizing the status quo if he thought there was a better way. In a gentle dig at popular hymn writers, he suggested they often started off with a good idea but wandered on from there until they lost sight of their original intention.

Montgomery, on the other hand, liked to find a powerful theme and stick with it. The idea that God would come to earth through Jesus Christ struck him as an awesome one, well worth rejoicing over. He left the theme for one stanza only, to tell what this miracle meant to humankind. Repentant sinners, he said, had been set free. Mercy had broken their chains.

An orphan boy who eventually became a newspaper owner, Montgomery found himself in chains more than once. His views on poverty, social conditions, and slavery earned him two spells of imprisonment in York Castle. Undaunted, he would go on to champion many causes that bettered the plight of the ordinary man and woman.

His earthly reward, for his reforms, his poetry, and his hymns, would eventually come in the form of a royal pension.

Asked which of his works would survive him, he replied in a way that clearly showed his priorities. "None, sir. Nothing except, perhaps, a few of my hymns." "Angels, from the Realms of Glory" is still sung all across the English-speaking world, more than a century and a half after his death.

Growing up without a family may have brought Montgomery closer to the realms of charity. Spending his childhood with no place to call home may have brought him closer to the realms of eternity. The day after completing his four hundredth hymn, at age eighty-three, he went to his real home and his heavenly family.

The angels must have rejoiced in the realms of glory when James Montgomery arrived.

*Praise ye him, all his angels: praise ye him, all his hosts.*
*Praise ye him, sun and moon: praise him, all ye stars of light.*
Psalm 148:2–3

# Angels, from the Realms of Glory

An-gels, from the realms of glo-ry, Wing your flight o'er all the earth;

Angels, from the realms of glory,
Wing your flight o'er all the earth.
Ye who sang creation's story,
Now proclaim Messiah's birth.

Come and worship. Come and worship.
Worship Christ, the newborn King.

Shepherds, in the field abiding,
Watching o'er your flocks by night,
God with man is now residing;
Yonder shines the Infant Light.

## Good Christian Men, Rejoice

Good Chris-tian men, re - joice    with heart and soul, and    voice;

Good Christian men, rejoice
With heart and soul and voice.
Give ye heed to what we say:
News! News!
Jesus Christ is born today!
Ox and ass before Him bow,
And He is in the manger now.
Christ is born today!
Christ is born today!

# Sweet Song of the Angels

Well, what would *you* do if you stumbled upon some angels having a sing-song? Henry Suso (no doubt after he had picked himself up from the floor) joined right in the singing and did a little dance for good measure. Then, once the angels were gone, he wrote down the lyrics.

Try taking that to a copyright lawyer!

Suso (or Heinrich Seuse) was a student of the German monk Meister Eckhart, and his angelic encounter is said to have taken place just before the song's publication in 1328.

"*In Dulci Jubilo*," the original title of the piece, means "In Sweetest Rejoicing." It concentrated on the wonder that was Christ's birth and what it meant for humankind. The music, by the same name, has to be one of the most recognizable of all Christmas melodies. J. S. Bach wrote a choral prelude around it, and Franz Liszt included it in his Weihnachtsbaum piano suite. Nearly 650 years after the song was first published, Mike Oldfield, composer of *Tubular Bells*, took the tune to number four on the British pop charts.

The Suso version of the song was written in Latin. In the early nineteenth century, English composer Robert Lucas de Pearsall widened the song's appeal by producing a version combining Latin and English lyrics. Shortly afterward the English hymn writer John Mason Neale "freely" adapted "In Dulci Jubilo" into "Good Christian Men, Rejoice" and gave the world the version we now know.

Neale's words differed considerably from the original, but in the spirit of the song, he deviated not at all. Both versions are full of wonder at the fact that Christ would be born for us—and would die to save us.

Suso's version mentions the joys to be found "*in Regis curia*" (in the King's court), and Neale has Jesus call us to "His everlasting hall." Whether the song is in Latin or English, the joy therein surely gives good Christian men and women cause to sing "in dulci jubilo," in sweetest rejoicing.

> *And thou shalt have joy and gladness;*
> *and many shall rejoice at his birth.*
> Luke 1:14

# The Fideles Code

Fans of books like *The Da Vinci Code* will appreciate the story behind the Christmas carol "O Come, All Ye Faithful."

Originally written in Latin as "*Adeste Fideles*," the origins of the piece are tantalizingly obscure. The lyrics may have originated in the thirteenth century, or they may have been written in the seventeenth century by a Portuguese king. But the best claim to authorship is held by the man who first published the hymn. John Francis Wade, a Jacobite sympathizer in exile in France, published his *Cantus Diversi,* including "Adeste Fidelus," in 1751.

A supporter of Bonnie Prince Charlie, who attempted to capture the British crown in 1745, Wade decorated his manuscript with imagery that held significance for the Jacobite "faithful."

According to the theory, "Bethlehem" was a well-known code word for England, and *angelorum* ("angels" in the hymn) would be replaced with *Anglorum,* meaning "English." So "born the king of angels" became "born the king of the English."

It is always possible that the song had a hidden meaning, but it's more likely that Wade, who also wrote other hymns, was a man of God celebrating the birth of his Savior.

Frederick Oakley, a canon at Westminster Cathedral, translated the first four verses into English, and William Brooke, a hymn writer, completed the job. The version modern carolers would recognize as "O Come, All Ye Faithful" appeared first in *Murray's Hymnal* in 1852. Since then it has been translated into more than 125 other languages.

Any political dimension, if there ever was one, has long since been rendered obsolete, and the song remains a firm favorite among the real faithful at Christmas.

So all the ingredients for a mystery are there. . .or are they? And even if the conspiracy theory *was* true, it wouldn't be the first time God had taken something worldly and turned it into something sublime.

*This is a great mystery: but I speak concerning Christ and the church.*
Ephesians 5:32

## O Come, All Ye Faithful

O come, all ye faithful,
Joyful and triumphant.
O come ye, O come ye to Bethlehem.
Come and behold Him—
Born the King of angels!
O come, let us adore Him!
O come, let us adore Him!
O come, let us adore Him—
Christ, the Lord!

## Infant Holy, Infant Lowly

In-fant  ho - ly.  In-fant  low - ly,  for His  bed  a  cat-tle  stall

Infant holy, Infant lowly,
For His bed a cattle stall.
Oxen lowing, little knowing
Christ, the Babe, is Lord of all.
Swift are winging angels singing,
Noels ringing, tidings bringing:
Christ, the Babe, is Lord of all!
Christ, the Babe, is Lord of all!

# The Greatest Mystery

"Infant Holy, Infant Lowly" sums up the contrasts in the life of Jesus Christ. How could He be both?

Originally a Polish hymn called "*W Zlobie Lezy*" or "He Lies in a Cradle," it was the work of Piotr Skarga, a sixteenth-century Jesuit priest. A man of contrasts himself, he founded a college, a pawnshop, and a bank, all for the aid of the poor, but still managed to be a major force in Poland's political history.

The music for the hymn reached England long before the text did, being attached to several other songs. It took a war to finally unite the music with an English version of Skarga's words. Two years after the end of World War I, perhaps influenced by the songs of displaced Poles, Edith Margaret Gellibrand Reed turned "W Zlobie Lezy" into "Infant Holy, Infant Lowly."

Edith Reed was a traveler and editor of music magazines. She also wrote mystery (or miracle) plays about the birth of Christ, exploring the "mystery" of God becoming man. The similarity between the plays and the hymn may have been what inspired her to work on the translation.

"Infant Holy, Infant Lowly" leaves listeners in no doubt that even though this child was born in the lowest of circumstances, He was still, mysteriously and miraculously, "the Lord of all." The Creator became part of His very own creation. And even though He came to save the whole world—well, He isn't going to do that in a straightforward way either. With the salvation of humankind as His holy mission, He, mysteriously and miraculously, has one lowly human as His priority. As the song says in its last line, "Christ the Babe was born for you."

*And the angel answered and said unto her,*
*The Holy Ghost shall come upon thee,*
*and the power of the Highest shall overshadow thee:*
*therefore also that holy thing which shall be born of thee*
*shall be called the Son of God.*
Luke 1:35

# The End of the Beginning

"Lo, He Comes with Clouds Descending" was very much a Methodist hymn—but no faith or denomination owns the copyright to beauty. Divinely inspired, songs like this become gifts to the whole world.

John Cennick, author of the original version, spent his early teens living the low life in London, gambling, lying, and stealing.

A meeting with John Wesley, a founder of the Methodists, turned Cennick's life around. Wesley found him a job and Cennick became the first Methodist lay preacher, though he would spend the greater part of his life founding Moravian churches in Ireland.

His meeting with John Wesley also introduced him to Charles, John's brother. The junior Wesley, a hugely prolific hymn writer, would take Cennick's hymn "Lo, He Comes with Countless Trumpets" and rewrite it as "Lo, He Comes with Clouds Descending." Charles Wesley published his version in *Hymns of Intercession for All Mankind* in 1758.

The hymn was changed yet again by Martin Madan, a young lawyer described as living "an uninhibited life." That is, until he, too, met John Wesley. Under Wesley's influence Madan became chaplain to Lock Hospital in London. The music played in his chapel made it quite the fashionable place to worship. In 1769 Madan published *The Lock Hospital Collection*, or *A Collection of Psalms and Hymns, Extracted from Various Authors*. In this volume he combined Cennick's hymn with Charles Wesley's and gave us the version we know today.

"Lo, He Comes with Clouds Descending" is very much a part of the Christmas repertoire these days, but it was originally a hymn of the Second Coming. When carolers sing, "God appears on earth to reign," they aren't referring to His first earthly appearance, but to His second.

While the Nativity is seen as the beginning of Jesus' story, "Lo, He Comes with Clouds Descending" celebrates the end. But, in true Messiah style, that ending is also a new and more wonderful beginning!

*And then shall they see the Son of man coming in the clouds*
*with great power and glory.*
Mark 13:26

## Lo, He Comes with Clouds Descending

**Lo!** He comes with clouds de - scend - ing,

Lo, He comes with clouds descending,
Once for favored sinners slain;
Thousand thousand saints attending
Swell the triumph of His train.
Hallelujah! Hallelujah!
God appears on earth to reign.

# The Birthday of a King

In the lit-tle vil-lage of Beth-le-hem, There lay a Child one day,

In the little village of Bethlehem,
There lay a Child one day,
And the sky was bright with a holy light
O'er the place where Jesus lay.

Alleluia! O how the angels sang!
Alleluia! How it rang!
And the sky was bright with a holy light;
'Twas the birthday of a King.

# The Once, Present, and Future King

How many kings have lived and died in the history of humankind? How many could you name? Countless kings have been welcomed into the world with processions, bands, and celebrations, only to have their reign end up as a footnote in an obscure history book or, worse, forgotten altogether.

A few of them might have been born in circumstances as humble as those of Jesus. Some of those would achieve great things. David was a shepherd boy who went on to have a long and glorious reign, but he knew his kingdom was a precursor to a greater one to come.

According to the terms by which we usually measure kings, Jesus achieved very little, but we still celebrate His birthday two thousand years later! Of course, He was a king before He was born and returned to a kingdom greater than any earthly empire after His death. His reign had, and will have, an eternal impact on the world.

In "The Birthday of a King," a song possibly written for children, William Harold Neidlinger explains the Nativity in the simplest of terms: The child was born and the angels sang because this child was, after all, a King unlike any other. The second, and last, verse is dedicated to how much God gave the world that day and the "perfect, holy way" Christ left behind.

We can visit historic castles and battlefields and pretend we are walking in the footsteps of some historic ruler, but we truly walk in Christ's footsteps, following that "perfect, holy way," each time we pray or hold out a helping hand in the name of Jesus.

Some more charitable monarchs give alms to the poor on their birthday. Christ's whole life was a gift—not just to the poor but to everyone who believes in Him.

He has had more than two thousand birthdays, and He's not finished yet. Now there's a King worth worshipping and a birthday worth celebrating!

*And as ye go, preach, saying, The kingdom of heaven is at hand.*
Matthew 10:7

Section 3:

Carols of Praise

## Good King Wenceslas

Good King Wen - ces - las looked out    on the Feast of    Ste - phen

Good King Wenceslas looked out
On the feast of Stephen,
When the snow lay round about,
Deep and crisp and even.
Brightly shone the moon that night,
Though the frost was cruel,
When a poor man came in sight,
Gathring winter fuel.

# Warmth in Winter

Good King Wenceslas wasn't a king in his lifetime—that honor was given after his death. But he was good enough to be fondly remembered by his people and made patron saint of the Czech Republic. From the balcony of his palace in Prague, tourists can still look out, as he did, over what is now Wenceslas Square.

Wenceslas was Duke of Bohemia in the tenth century. The carol telling of his exploits makes no reference to the Nativity—it's only sung at Christmas because it mentions Saint Stephen's feast, which falls on December 26.

Wenceslas, however, was a fine embodiment of the struggle between Christianity and paganism. His grandmother was Christian, while his mother held pagan beliefs. This dispute actually led to the younger woman murdering the older—but the grandmother's influence won the battle and Wenceslas grew up a devout Christian.

The carol tells of his mission to take food, drink, and firewood to a peasant family on the bleakest of winter nights. Legend has it that the duke often made such missions of mercy, usually walking barefoot to keep himself humble.

Humble or not, he was still a duke—and his servant probably did the bulk of the carrying. In the carol we hear how the boy's strength starts to give out and he fears he can't go on. Wenceslas tells the boy to walk in the footsteps he himself has left in the snow. Doing so, the servant not only finds the going easier but is sustained and strengthened by a mysterious warmth left behind by the duke's feet.

In his charitable mission Wenceslas embodies Christ's care for those in need. His servant might be said to be each of us—inasmuch as we often want to help but doubt our own abilities. Just like that humble servant, we find strength to do more than we ever thought we could—when we walk in the footsteps of our Lord.

*If any man serve me, let him follow me; and where I am,*
*there shall also my servant be: if any man serve me,*
*him will my Father honour.*
John 12:26

# In Every Language

Some carols are hard to pin down, and that is part of their charm! Once upon a time there was a popular "hunting tune" in the region of Normandy. It was already an old composition when it first appeared in print in 1862. To that tune some unknown wordsmith added the lyrics to "*Il Est Ne, Le Divin Enfant*," and the completed carol made its debut in *Noêls Anciens* fourteen years later.

However, there are many versions of the lyrics, and without an author's signature, none of them can be proven to be the original.

In one version the birth of Christ is celebrated with oboes and bagpipes. In another the instruments are the oboe and the musette. "Gaily resounding pipe and drum" accompany the Nativity in a third version, and a fourth has the oboe vying with the bagpipes for the honor of proclaiming the birth.

The time we have waited for this momentous event might be "long ages of the past" or "four thousand years."

Some versions mention the manger, the shepherds, and the star, while others focus more on what His blessed birth means to the world.

The hymn is sung at different tempos and with varying lyrics all across the world. There is even rumored to be a Native American version sung by the Mohawk people.

The heart of the hymn, whether it is "Il Est Ne, Le Divin Enfant," or "He Is Born, the Divine Christ Child," or (in Mohawk) "*Rotonni Niio Roienha*," remains one of rejoicing that Christ was born for us.

This tremendous variety wrapped around the same essential message reflects well the people who sing it. Human beings come in a variety of shapes and sizes, using many different languages, but the central theme running through all those hearts is one of yearning for God.

So grab your bagpipes, oboes, pipes, drums, or whatever your instrument of choice is, and make a joyous noise because that divine Christ child—He is born for everyone!

*Speaking to yourselves in psalms and hymns and spiritual songs,*
*singing and making melody in your heart to the Lord.*
Ephesians 5:19

# He Is Born, the Divine Christ Child

He is born, the di - vine Christ child, Play on the o - boe and

He is born, the divine Christ child.
Play on the oboe and bagpipes merrily.
He is born, the divine Christ child.
Sing we all of the Saviour's birth.

Through long ages of the past,
Prophets have foretold His coming;
Through long ages of the past,
Now the time has come at last.

# Hark, the Herald Angels Sing

Hark! the her - ald an - gels sing, "Glo - ry to the new - born Ki

Hark! the herald angels sing,
"Glory to the newborn King!
Peace on earth, and mercy mild—
God and sinners reconciled."
Joyful, all ye nations rise;
Join the triumph of the skies.
With the angelic host proclaim,
"Christ is born in Bethlehem!"
Hark! the herald angels sing,
"Glory to the newborn King."

# The Welkin Chorus

"Hark! the Herald Angels Sing" manages to mix respectful sobriety with joyful exultation, perhaps reflecting the attitude toward worship held by its author, Charles Wesley.

Charles, the brother of John Wesley, was known to be a serious fellow, but his delight in the Lord can be found in the seven thousand hymns he is supposed to have written!

"Hark! the Herald Angels Sing" first appeared in *Hymns and Sacred Poems* in 1739. *The History and Use of Hymns and Hymn Tunes*, a nineteenth-century compilation by Rev. James King, proclaimed it one of the four great Anglican hymns. Two of those four came from Charles Wesley's pen, with the other one being, "Lo, He Comes with Clouds Descending."

Originally the hymn began, "Hark! how all the welkin rings. Glory to the King of Kings." The *welkin*, a term not much used these days, was the celestial sphere, the heavens, the afterlife, basically everything that wasn't this earth. And it *all* rejoiced!

George Whitefield, sometimes a colleague of the Wesleys, changed those lines and gave the world the version sung today. But still, it was only sung in praise meetings and to a far more sedate tune.

A hundred years after Wesley wrote the hymn, Felix Mendelssohn composed a cantata for the anniversary of—appropriately—the invention of the printing press. Part of this piece was adapted for "Hark! the Herald Angels Sing," and the two have been printed together ever since. Mendelssohn's music helped the piece make the transition from hymn to carol.

Wesley's words moved out onto the streets at Christmas, reminding everyone that through His Son, God became reconciled with sinners. Unfortunately, not all sinners choose to reconcile with God. So the faithful still have work to do.

In singing joyful hymns and living godly lives, we continue that work, making each of us a herald of the good news. So let's join with Charles Wesley *and* the angels in lovingly proclaiming, "Glory to the newborn King!"

*And the angel answering said unto him,*
*I am Gabriel, that stand in the presence of God;*
*and am sent to speak unto thee, and to shew thee these glad tidings.*
Luke 1:19

# Mysterious Ways, Unexpected People

"O Holy Night" is faith in full poetic flower. It tells how lost the world was before Christ came; it reminds us "His law is love and His gospel is peace"; it makes falling to our knees seem less like submission and more like coming home.

So it comes as a surprise to learn that the author, Placide Cappeau de Roquemaure, was not a devout man of God. He was a nineteenth-century wine merchant who attended church sporadically and later gave it up altogether.

When a priest asked him to write a poem for Christmas, de Roquemaure came up with "*Cantique de Noel.*" So impressed was he by it that he asked a friend to set it to music. His friend, composer Adolphe-Charles Adam, may have been a man of God. He was also Jewish.

The priest loved the end result, and the hymn rapidly became a favorite in French churches. But when its provenance was discovered, the French establishment declared it unfit for church use.

Ten years later, in 1857, John Sullivan Dwight translated it for an American audience. Abolitionists heard the lines "Chains shall He break, for the slave is our brother; and in His name all oppression shall cease," and they adopted the song as an anthem for their struggle.

Preempting the Christmas truce of World War I, a French soldier in the Franco-Prussian war leapt from his trench on Christmas Eve 1871. He stood, unarmed, in no-man's-land and serenaded the enemy with "O Holy Night."

On Christmas Eve 1906, Reginald Fessenden made what may well have been the first radio broadcast of speech and music. He quoted from the Gospel of Luke (on which de Roquemaure based his poem), then took out his violin and played "O Holy Night" to the world.

The message of that "night divine" is still being spread, in the most surprising ways and by the most unexpected people.

*And the angel said unto them, Fear not: for, behold,*
*I bring you good tidings of great joy, which shall be to all people.*
Luke 2:10

## O Holy Night

O holy night,
the stars are brightly shining;
It is the night of our dear Savior's birth.
Long lay the world in sin and error pining,
Till He appeared and the soul felt its worth.
A thrill of hope—the weary world rejoices,
For yonder breaks a new and glorious morn!
Fall on your knees! O hear the angel voices!
O night divine!
O night when Christ was born!
O night divine! O night, O night divine!

## While Sheperds Watched Their Flocks

While shep-herds watched their flocks by night, All   seat-ed on the gro

While shepherds watched
Their flocks by night,
All seated on the ground,
The angel of the Lord came down,
And glory shone around,
And glory shone around.

"Fear not," said he,
For mighty dread
Had seized their troubled mind.
"Glad tidings of great joy I bring
To you and all mankind,
To you and all mankind."

# With Luke as a Lyric

These days we have a wonderful array of hymns and carols to sing at Christmas. Imagine if there was only one!

Between the years 1700 and 1782, "While Shepherds Watched Their Flocks" was the only Christmas hymn authorized to be sung by the Anglican Church. Prior to 1700 only the psalms of David were permitted to be sung in church, and melodies had to be twisted around the words. Several writers worked at changing this tradition, and as England's sixth poet laureate, Nahum Tate had more influence than many.

In 1696 Tate and Nicholas Brady (chaplain to King William II and Queen Anne) produced their *New Version of the Psalms of David,* adapting the psalms to make them easier to sing. The differences weren't great, but this was still a momentous achievement for their time.

In 1702 Tate and Brady produced a supplement to their book that contained the hymn "While Shepherds Watched Their Flocks." Based on the Gospel of Luke, it doesn't vary greatly from Luke 2:8–14. Doubtless Tate did not want to be too revolutionary!

With music written from Handel's 1728 opera *Siroe,* adapted by American composer Lowell Mason, "While Shepherds Watched Their Flocks" is the only composition from Tate and Brady's supplement still sung today.

The son of an Irish vicar, Tate moved to London in an attempt to make a living as a poet. In becoming poet laureate he made it to the very pinnacle of his chosen profession. Unfortunately, he died at age sixty-three while claiming sanctuary in the Royal Mint, a man deeply in debt and pursued by his creditors. Thankfully he left this world a classic carol announcing the birth of "the heavenly Babe" before passing on to a realm where he would find that all his debts were already forgiven.

*The LORD is my shepherd; I shall not want.*
*He maketh me to lie down in green pastures:*
*he leadeth me beside the still waters.*
Psalm 23:1–2

# An Open Invitation—RSVP

Emily Elliott (1836–1897) surely would have had plenty of encouragement with her early hymn writing ventures. After all, she had an uncle and two aunts who both wrote hymns, and her father was rector of an Anglican church in Brighton, England.

Still, it would take passionate faith instead of simple encouragement to produce, as she did, 140 hymns in her lifetime.

Elliott's passion for the Lord was obvious and bent to a purpose—the purpose of helping the poor and the dispossessed. Her life was spent in rescue missions and benevolent associations. Her care for the infirm is shown in a book of verse, *Under the Pillow*, which she wrote exclusively to comfort those who were bedridden.

Elliot was also very involved with the relatively new Sunday school movement, providing literacy skills, religious education, and, in many cases, food and clothing to children in major industrial centers.

It was for some of these children that Elliott wrote "Thou Didst Leave Thy Throne," based on Luke's Gospel. Despite publishing several books and no doubt earning an income from them, Elliot had "Thou Didst Leave Thy Throne" published privately for the children at the Sunday school of her father's church. It was an attempt to show, in simple terms, the extent of the sacrifice that was Christ's life.

Elliot's hymn left the children in no doubt that Christ wasn't angry, in spite of having visited humanity and been repaid with scorn and a crown of thorns. Indeed, there would come a day when He would call out to each of them and invite them to come stand by His side. For the hungry, ill-educated, and short-lived children of the Industrial Revolution that must have been a wondrous invitation.

Of course, others thought so, too, and the hymn didn't long remain exclusively with her father's church. An invitation like that was meant to travel the world, and here's the good news—it still stands!

*In my Father's house are many mansions: if it were not so,*
*I would have told you. I go to prepare a place for you.*
John 14:2

# Thou Didst Leave Thy Throne

Thou didst leave Thy throne and Thy king - ly crown, When Thou

Thou didst leave Thy throne
and Thy kingly crown
When Thou camest to earth for me;
But in Bethlehem's home
there was found no room
For Thy holy nativity.
O come to my heart, Lord Jesus;
There is room in my heart for Thee.

## For Unto Us a Child Is Born

For un-to us a Child is born, un-to us a Son is giv-

For unto us a Child is born,
Unto us a Son is given,
And the government shall be
upon His shoulder,
And His Name shall be called
Wonderful, Counsellor,
The Mighty God, the Everlasting Father,
The Prince of Peace.

# The Master of Effects

Recalling the creation of his masterpiece *Messiah*, George Frideric Handel said, "I saw the heavens opened. . .and God sitting on the throne. . .whether I was in my body or out of my body when I wrote it I know not. God knows."

His oratorio, from which "For unto Us a Child Is Born" and "I Know My Redeemer Liveth" come, was written at a phenomenal pace, probably in the country home of Charles Jennings, the author of the libretto. From start to finish, Handel's composition of the music for *Messiah* took just twenty-four days in the summer of 1741. Jennings's words drew heavily from the Bible, telling the story of Jesus Christ from His anticipation to His glorification. "For unto Us a Child Is Born" comes from Isaiah 9:6 with additions by Jennings.

The collaboration with Jennings came at a low point in Handel's career, but such was the inspiration found in the words that the composer (so legend has it) could be heard weeping as he worked.

Despite opposition to the Lord's words being performed in London theaters, *Messiah* was quickly reckoned to be the greatest composition ever. Early performances were held in aid of debtors' prisons and orphanages, enabling the delighted press to write that the *Messiah* had "fed the hungry, clothed the naked, and fostered the orphan."

Handel's music was held in such high esteem that Bach, Beethoven, and Mozart all admired him. Beethoven described him as musically "the master of us all" and advised students to "go to him to learn how to achieve great effects, by such simple means."

Master of this technique though he was, Handel surely would have considered himself a novice next to God. After all, the birth of a child has to be the simplest of all means, but what "great effects" that had!

*And the child grew, and waxed strong in spirit, filled with wisdom: and the grace of God was upon him.*
Luke 2:40

# Songs of Suffering and Joy

If any one group could identify with the suffering of the Jewish people during their time of exile, it would be the people taken from Africa and sold into generations of slavery. It's little wonder that, lacking any other support, those slaves, in the fields and homes of their owners, turned to God for love and redemption.

A rich tradition of gospel songs sprang from the fertile ground of their suffering, but theirs was not a lifestyle that allowed for the writing of music or the copying down of songs. Who knows how many praise-filled melodies came and were lost for the lack of a pen and an interested listener?

In the nineteenth and twentieth centuries, John Wesley Work tried to remedy the situation. Graduating in 1895 from Fisk (at the time a university predominantly dedicated to the education of freed slaves and their children), Work went on to head the school's Latin and history departments.

While teaching there he became interested in collecting and promoting Negro spirituals. He and his brother Jerome published a collection called *New Jubilee Songs as Sung by the Fisk Jubilee Singers* in 1901. This was followed six years later by *Folk Songs of the American Negro*, which included "Go, Tell It on the Mountain."

Lacking Bibles, the dispossessed traditionally tended to rely on rhythmic songs, easy to sing while working and containing messages powerful enough to get them to the end of the day. "Go, Tell It on the Mountain" is a simple recounting of the Nativity story with the star, shepherds, manger, and Baby— and it ends with the assurance of salvation.

The chorus reminds the listener that this is a message worth singing not just in the fields and valleys but from the tops of the highest mountains.

The slaves told the story in song, and John Wesley Work heard it. He told us. Now whom can we tell?

*The word which God sent unto the children of Israel,*
*preaching peace by Jesus Christ: (he is Lord of all).*
Acts 10:36

## Go, Tell It on the Mountain

Go, tell it on the moun-tain, O-ver the hills and ev - ery-where

Go, tell it on the mountain,
Over the hills and everywhere;
Go, tell it on the mountain
That Jesus Christ is born!

Angels We Have heard on High

An-gels we have heard on high    Sweet-ly sing-ing o'er the plain

Angels we have heard on high,
Sweetly singing o'er the plains,
And the mountains in reply,
Echoing their joyous strains.
Gloria, in excelsis Deo!
Gloria, in excelsis Deo!

# Sing the Song of the Angels

"Angels We Have Heard on High" was originally the traditional French tune *"Les Angeles dans Nos Campagnes,"* which translates as "Angels in Our Countryside." The angels in question weren't in any European countryside, though—they were in the hills around Bethlehem, telling the shepherds the good news.

Legend has it that the French shepherds took this part of Luke's Gospel to heart, and they would sing the Nativity story on the hills around Christmastime. Perhaps it was purely for the joy of worship, or perhaps it was simply a way of letting the shepherds on the other side of the valley or on neighboring hills know they were not alone. These were, of course, the days before cell phones! The song they sang is reputed to have evolved into "Les Angeles dans Nos Campagnes."

It's a simple but joyful telling of that angelic visit on the night of the Savior's birth. The hills resound with the angels' chorus; then the shepherds sing it to the world. When others ask them what all the noise is about, they reply, "Come to Bethlehem and see!"

In 1862, four years before he became bishop of Hexham and Newcastle in England, James Chadwick translated the traditional French carol into "Angels We Have Heard on High." It first appeared in print in *Holy Family Hymns.* The tune we know came later, adapted by American Edwin Shippen Barnes, who studied music in France and may have heard the original version there.

Just as God didn't hesitate to become man, so humankind shouldn't hesitate to sing the songs of praise the angels sang. When it comes to *"Gloria, in excelsis deo"* (or "Glory to God in the highest"), you don't need wings to sing. You just need what those French shepherds must have had—a good strong pair of lungs.

*And when they had seen it, they made known abroad the saying*
*which was told them concerning this child.*
*And all they that heard it wondered at those things*
*which were told them by the shepherds.*

Luke 2:17–18

# Sing Salvation to the Angels

Most translations of the Bible say the angels *spoke* praises to the Lord while the shepherds stood listening in fear and awe. But the image of a heavenly choir *singing* as Jesus is born persists. Why? Perhaps it's because such wonderful news inspires the human heart to something more exuberant than speaking.

Think about it. The Creator of all things came down to be among us, and He wasn't angry with us—He had come to love and save us! If the angels *weren't* singing, it might be because they had never been lost; they had never needed saving. Humanity, on the other hand, would have felt the loss more keenly and celebrated salvation more rapturously.

Josiah G. Holland sticks with the tradition of the song from on high in his poem "There's a Song in the Air," first published in his book *The Marble Prophecy and Other Poems* in 1872. A doctor, teacher, novelist, poet, journalist, and editor, Holland was a friend of Emily Dickinson and wrote a well-received biography of President Lincoln.

A glance through *The Marble Prophecy* shows that faith loomed large in Holland's life. Indeed, he followed the Methodist tradition, as did Karl Harrington, who, two years after Holland died, took the words of his poem "There's a Song in the Air" and put them to music.

The angelic serenade may be the starting point to this beautiful Christmas carol, but then Holland describes how the song sweeps around the world and still blazes in the hearth of each Christian home. Angels didn't do that. People, walking with the Holy Spirit and with hearts full of joy at their redemption, did.

The angels may or may not have sung the first *"Gloria in excelsis"* on that holy night. But, as Holland points out in the last stanza of "There's a Song in the Air," the children of the Lord have been singing it back to them ever since.

*Sing unto the LORD, all the earth;*
*shew forth from day to day his salvation.*
1 Chronicles 16:23

There's a song in the air! There's a star in the sky!

There's a song in the air;
There's a star in the sky.
There's a mother's deep prayer
And a Baby's low cry.
And the star rains its fire
While the beautiful sing,
For the manger of Bethlehem
Cradles a King!

Section 4:

Carols of Mystery

# Better Times Ahead

William Chatterton Dix wasn't having a good time. Twenty-nine and far from home, he'd been seriously ill for months. His position as a Glasgow maritime insurance clerk must have been in jeopardy. He had every right to be depressed—and he was!

Even so, he kept his mind on better things. While confined to bed, Dix wrote several poems that would become hymns we still sing a century and a half later.

"What Child Is This?" was composed in 1865 and appeared in *Christmas Carols New and Old* six years later. By then it had been associated with the tune "Greensleeves."

The carol begins with a question, but there is no uncertainty in Dix's answer. "This, this," he repeats, "is Christ the King"—and we should rush to praise Him.

Why? Well, the illustration on the sheet music from *Christmas Carols New and Old* tells what that child would go through. In a simple pen and ink sketch we see Mary and Joseph watching over their new baby. Beneath the sketch, we see what awaits their beloved son: the scourge, the spear, the sponge of vinegar, the crown of thorns, and the nails.

But Dix's words take the story further. The child's humble beginnings do not lead only to a mean and miserable death. This baby, laid in a manger, would be the King of salvation for everyone. He would go from the cross to rule in the hearts of peasants and kings alike. He would reign in heaven—and invite us in!

In his illness and depression, stuck in his lodgings with money running out, Dix was certain there was better to come. Why? Because Mary's child, in a world that was not *His* home, had already gone through far worse to ensure there was better to come for everyone.

*Now the birth of Jesus Christ was on this wise:*
*When as his mother Mary was espoused to Joseph,*
*before they came together, she was found with child of the Holy Ghost.*
Matthew 1:18

## What Child Is This?

What Child is this who, laid to rest On Ma-ry's lap is sleep-ing?

What Child is this who, laid to rest,
On Mary's lap is sleeping?
Whom angels greet with anthems sweet,
While shepherds watch are keeping?
This, this is Christ, the King,
Whom shepherds guard and angels sing.
Haste, haste to bring Him laud,
The Babe, the Son of Mary.

## Coventry Carol

Lul-ly, lul-lay, Thou lit-tle ti-ny Child, By, by, lul-ly, lul-l

Lullay, Thou little tiny Child,
Bye, bye, lully, lullay.
Lullay, Thou little tiny Child.
Bye, bye, lully, lullay.

O sisters, too, how may we do,
For to preserve this day;
This poor Youngling for whom we sing,
Bye, bye, lully, lullay.

# A "Child for Thee"

Many carols get criticized for focusing on the party aspect of Christmas without ever mentioning Christ or the salvation He brought to the world. "Coventry Carol" might be seen as equally remiss—but it is far from a party song.

It focuses on an aspect of the Nativity often overlooked in the celebrations. The major character is King Herod, which gives a big hint as to the subject matter.

First written down by Robert Croo in 1533, the carol dates from the previous century and was part of the mystery plays performed in the English town of Coventry. The "mystery" here was not of the whodunit type; rather, it concerned the mystery of Christ's birth, death, and resurrection. These plays were often performed on wagons in the streets with the actors changing underneath.

The somber subject of this particular play was the massacre of the innocents by a vengeful King Herod.

Jesus and His family escaped Herod's wrath by fleeing to Egypt, but Herod had many children and babies put to the sword in the hope of killing the Messiah. "Coventry Carol" is sung from the point of view of young Bethlehem mothers, shushing their babies in the forlorn hope that the soldiers would pass by. Sadly, they didn't.

The "lully, lullay" with which the mothers soothed their children may have gone on to become our modern *lullaby*. In the carol, it soon turns to "woe is me."

Those little ones are still remembered in *Childermas*, or the Feast Day of the Innocents, celebrated on the twenty-eighth of December.

The haunting tones of "Coventry Carol" are a reminder that the first Christmas, though a time of joy, was dearly bought—and is all the more precious because of it.

*Then Herod, when he saw that he was mocked of the wise men,*
*was exceeding wroth, and sent forth, and slew all the children*
*that were in Bethlehem, and in all the coasts thereof,*
*from two years old and under, according to the time*
*which he had diligently inquired of the wise men.*
Matthew 2:16

# Ships in the Desert

Some carols seem designed to have us scratching our heads. "I Saw Three Ships" is one of them. Ships sailing into Bethlehem? They would have to cross many miles of dry land first!

The origins of the song and its author are lost in history. Some claim the tune is merely a more upbeat version of "Greensleeves." Legend has Henry VIII as the author of that particular song.

"I Saw Three Ships" made its first appearance in print in John Forbes's *Cantus* in 1666. By the beginning of the twentieth century, Cecil Sharp, a collector of English folk songs, found there were many different versions being sung around the country.

One referred to "New Year's Day in the morning"; another sang about guests coming to a wedding. In some versions the occupants of the ships were "our Savior Christ and His Lady." In others the sailors were Joseph and Mary or simply three pretty girls; "One could whistle and one could sing. The other could play on the violin."

The three ships themselves have variously been thought to be Columbus's fleet; faith, hope, and charity; or the camels of the three wise men.

The apparent nonsense of the content and the repetition of the lyrics have caused the carol to be seen as a children's song. It is much likelier that the "nonsense" is actually complex symbolism, the key to which has been lost.

None of the above should detract from the pleasure found in singing a happy, upbeat carol. Where believers are gathered together to sing in celebration to their Lord, the lyrics are surely of secondary importance.

Except, perhaps, the ones that say, "And all the souls on earth shall sing on Christmas Day in the morning."

*Now when Jesus was born in Bethlehem of Judaea in the days*
*of Herod the king, behold, there came wise men from the east to*
*Jerusalem, saying, Where is he that is born King of the Jews?*
*for we have seen his star in the east, and are come to worship him.*
Matthew 2:1–2

## I Saw Three Ships

I saw three ships come sail-ing in On Christ-mas day, on Christ-mas day;

I saw three ships come sailing in
On Christmas Day, on Christmas Day;
I saw three ships come sailing in
On Christmas Day in the morning.

The Twelve Days of Christmas

On the first day of Christ-mas my true love sent to me

On the first day of Christmas,
My true love sent to me
A partridge in a pear tree.

On the second day of Christmas,
My true love sent to me
Two turtledoves,
And a partridge in a pear tree.

# What Did Santa Bring You?

We rightly worry that Christmas might be too much about fun and games and not enough about Christ—but that doesn't mean fun and games should be done away with! "The Twelve Days of Christmas" is one of the season's most enjoyable carols. Not only does it take strong lungs and good breath control; it's also a workout for the memory.

The intentions of the original writer are lost in history. Appearing in print for the first time in eighteenth-century England, "The Twelve Days of Christmas" is much older and probably French in origin. Since then different cultures have reinterpreted the gifts or even replaced the originals with presents that fit better locally.

Much of the original sense has been lost or misinterpreted over the centuries. "Calling birds" may originally have been "colly" or "coal-y" birds, that is, birds as black as coal—blackbirds. The famous "five golden rings" weren't jewelry; they were probably "ring-necked" pheasants. The pear tree the partridge perches in on the first day might be a corruption of *perdrix*, pronounced "per-dree," which is simply French for "partridge"!

Devoid of any spiritual meaning or reference to the Nativity, "The Twelve Days of Christmas" may have been intended to be sung *after* Christmas in the twelve days between Boxing Day and the Feast of the Epiphany. Christmas Day itself would rightly be a time for devotions. Present giving might then continue right up to the big party on twelfth night. Then partygoers might recount all the presents they had received and challenge others to recite their lists—to music!

Legend has the song being a religious code for those persecuted under the reign of England's Henry VIII, but human nature sometimes creates a mystery where there is no obvious explanation.

In the end, "The Twelve Days of Christmas" may simply be a game, a fun song for the whole company. Surely there's a place for that at Christmas, too.

*Now there are diversities of gifts, but the same Spirit.*
1 Corinthians 12:4

# An Everlasting Light

Is it "Noel" or "*Nowell*"? That depends on whether you were living in France in the sixteenth century, or a few miles across the Channel in England at the same time. Both countries were keen on "mystery" plays, dramatizing and putting to music the mystery of Christ's birth.

Basically, the spelling of that old word for Christmas depended on which king the singers lived under. Such was the rivalry between France and England that they might have separate kings or be ruled by a king across the water. After William of Normandy's dramatic 1066 victory, the spelling was finalized. It would be "Noel" in the language of the ruling elite.

Ironically, the song in question celebrated the birth of the king who would make all others redundant and end the divisions of language and nationality.

In the tradition of the mystery play, "The First Noel" faithfully recounts the story of the star, the birth, the shepherds, and the wise men. In 1833 William B. Sandys put the words and music into print in his *Christmas Carols Ancient and Modern*. It may have been he who added the often omitted last verse, "If we in our time shall do well, we shall be free from death and hell, for God hath prepared for us all a resting-place in general."

The carol is English, probably Cornish, but the word *Noel* is of French origin. It may have come from the Latin *natalis*, meaning "birth," but it is more likely to have come from the ancient Gaulish term *neu helle*. The pagan Gauls used *neu helle* to refer to the winter solstice and the coming of the sun. It means "new light."

When the faithful get to that "resting-place in general," they will undoubtedly find that the new light of Jesus Christ still shines just as brightly as it did all those centuries ago—on that first noel.

*And, behold, thou shalt conceive in thy womb,*
*and bring forth a son, and shalt call his name JESUS.*
Luke 1:31

## The First Noel

The first Noel the angels did say
Was to certain poor shepherds
in fields as they lay—
In fields where they lay keeping their sheep
On a cold winter's night that was so deep.
Noel, Noel, Noel, Noel!
Born is the King of Israel!

# The Holly and the Ivy

The hol-ly and the i-vy, when they are both full grown

The holly and the ivy,
When they are both full grown,
Of all the trees that are in the wood,
The holly bears the crown.
O the rising of the sun,
And the running of the deer,
The playing of the merry organ,
Sweet singing of the choir.

# The Contest for the Crown

As Christianity spread throughout the world, it adopted and adapted many of the customs it came across. Sometimes this was very problematic; other times less so. Many pagan beliefs elevated aspects of creation. Christianity gave pagan people a Creator, a reason behind the wonders and marvels they worshipped.

"The Holly and the Ivy" takes elements of the natural world already revered by Druidic societies and lightly compares them to the birth of Christ. It's a gentle marrying of two traditions, one older but the other far more significant. The partnership continues in the happy repetition of pagan images likening running deer and the midwinter sun alongside Christian images of organ music and choral singing.

"The Holly and the Ivy" is first mentioned in print in 1710, but the song itself may be more than a thousand years old. Undoubtedly English, it is thought to have originated in the Somerset and Gloucester area.

While both holly and ivy were known for their ability to survive even the harshest winters and for their possible medicinal value, in many cultures the former actually symbolizes masculinity while the latter represents femininity.

An early version of the song reinforces this idea in what it calls "the contest between the Holly and the Ivy." In this version the holly is indoors, plainly master of the house, while the ivy hangs around the door weeping and wishing she could come in.

Perhaps the contest is still reflected in the modern carol where it says that "the holly bears the crown"—but it must be remembered that the crown was a crown of thorns. The red berries adorning it represent the drops of blood on Christ's brow.

The contest between men and women may continue. But as we sing, may it be true that the real master of all our houses is not the man—but the Son of Man!

*Then came Jesus forth, wearing the crown of thorns,*
*and the purple robe. And Pilate saith unto them,*
*Behold the man!*
John 19:5

# The Midwinter Flower

If you believe God is Lord of all, then it follows that nothing happens by accident.

"Lo, How a Rose E'er Blooming" has journeyed through religious upheavals and been written or rewritten by more than seven different composers. Add to that the fact that the "Rose" in the title originally referred to Mary, not Jesus, and the "*ros*" referred to may have been a "*reis*" or sprig (or branch), and you might expect the confused remains of a holy song. Instead, what you get is a much-loved Christmas carol, beautifully come into its own.

"*Es Ist Ein Ros Entsprungen*" first appeared in either 1582 or 1588 in *Gebetbuchlein des Frater Conradus*. Originally it contained nineteen verses dedicated to Mary, the mother of Christ. Its composer may have been an anonymous monk who, walking in the woods on Christmas Eve, found a midwinter rose.

Martin Luther wanted to downplay Mary's role and refocus on Christ. Michael Praetorius, a Lutheran hymn writer, harmonized and recorded the hymn in his 1609 *Muses of Zion*, changing the focus to Jesus (a "branch" or "reis" from the stump of Jesse).

In 1844 Freidrich Leyritz reissued the song after changing the third and fourth stanzas so that both Catholic and Protestant worshippers might feel comfortable singing it. New York–born Theodore Baker translated the first two stanzas from the original German in 1894, and Harriet Reynolds Kraugh seems to have given us the English version we have now.

With so many edits and alterations made to please different sides, the hymn ought to have fallen into obscurity long ago. Of course, God planned it differently. He wanted us to hear that long-ago monk's message: that Christ was "true man, yet very God," that He would flower brightest in the winter of our need, and that He will lead us to the "bright courts of heaven and to the endless day."

Then we will all be in full bloom.

*And there shall come forth a rod out of the stem of Jesse,*
*and a Branch shall grow out of his roots.*
Isaiah 11:1

# Lo, How a Rose E'er Blooming

Lo, how a Rose e'er bloom-ing from ten-der stem hath sprung.

Lo, how a Rose e'er blooming
from tender stem hath sprung!
Of Jesse's lineage coming,
as men of old have sung.
It came, a floweret bright,
amid the cold of winter,
When half spent was the night.

# O Come, O Come, Emmanuel

O come, O come, Em - man - u - el, And ran-som cap-

O come, O come, Emmanuel,
And ransom captive Israel,
That mourns in lowly exile here
Until the Son of God appear.
Rejoice! Rejoice! Emmanuel
Shall come to thee, O Israel!

# Ours for the Asking

The nation of Israel had never known a worse time. Its leaders were "guests" of a foreign power, and its people, all bar those needed to work the land and pay the tributes, had been exiled from their homeland, scattered as slaves throughout the Babylonian Empire.

What a fall this must have been for a people who thought themselves the favorites of the one God. Under David, a God-fearing king, Israel had been the local superpower. Now their nation barely existed. Where had it all gone wrong?

Well, the Old Testament prophets weren't slow in telling them. They had been proud, neglecting their Lord and worshipping other gods. He had turned away from them.

"O Come, O Come, Emmanuel" is sung from the point of view of the exiles, longing for God to be with them again. It's a nineteenth-century translation by John Mason Neal of the twelfth-century Latin text "*Veni, Veni, Emmanuel.*"

But it's not for nothing people say that God's mercy endures forever. Even in the depths of his disappointment with the Israelites, He sent word through His prophets that better times were to come. A Savior, the "Rod of Jesse" (in other words, a descendant of King David), would come to set them free.

The mournful longing in "O Come, O Come, Emmanuel" doubtless arises from the absolute assurance that their people would be redeemed—but not quickly. There was a lesson to be learned first!

Even today the faithful can fall, wrong turns can be taken, and it might seem as if God has looked away in annoyance. But the wonder of His love means He will always come back if we ask Him to. The timing will be *His* to decide—but it will be perfect.

Emmanuel means "God with us." If we ask Him to, God will *always* be with us!

> *Therefore the Lord himself shall give you a sign; Behold,*
> *a virgin shall conceive, and bear a son,*
> *and shall call his name Immanuel.*
>
> Isaiah 7:14

Section 5:

Carols of Joy

# Once in Royal David's City

Once in roy-al Da-vid's cit-y Stood a low-ly cat-tle she

Once in royal David's city
Stood a lowly cattle shed,
Where a mother laid her Baby
In a manger for His bed.
Mary was that mother mild—
Jesus Christ, her little Child.

# "Our Childhood's Pattern"—Always

The city in this carol isn't mighty Jerusalem where King David ruled so wisely for so long. It's the smaller but no less significant Bethlehem, where both David and Jesus were born.

Cecil Frances Humphreys, the daughter of a British army major based in Dublin, first told this story in her third book, *Hymns for Little Children*, which was published in 1848. As well as "Once in Royal David's City," the book contained two other works by Humphreys that would go on to wider acclaim: "All Things Bright and Beautiful" and "There Is a Green Hill Far Away." Perhaps unsurprisingly, the book was reprinted sixty-nine times in the next fifty-two years.

Humphreys married Rev. William Alexander two years after the publication of *Hymns for Little Children*. The reverend, also a poet, would go on to become the bishop of Derry in Northern Ireland.

As Mrs. Alexander, she dedicated her life to supporting her husband, writing hymns and poetry, and performing charitable work. Ironically, the beautiful hymns she wrote helped children who would never hear them. Proceeds from the sales of her earlier publications helped found a school for deaf and mute children. The sales of *Hymns for Little Children* would help maintain it.

"Once in Royal David's City" has traveled far from its beginning in Ireland and is now a firm favorite all around the world. Classifying it as a children's carol should not deter any adult from enjoying its pleasures. It's true that the author focuses on the town where David and Jesus were children and she uses the infant Christ as an example of how all good Christian children should behave. But she would have known that Jesus wanted us to come to Him as children and in the presence of the Father—well, what else would we want to be?

*For unto you is born this day in the city of David a Saviour,*
*which is Christ the Lord.*
Luke 2:11

# No Less Joyful

William Chatterton Dix came from an educated, literary English family—but that didn't mean they could provide a life of leisure for their children. As soon as he was old enough, Dix took employment in a Glasgow-based marine insurance company, hardly the most creative of environments.

Perhaps the monotonous nature of his work contributed to the periods of illness and depression he suffered. But amazingly, these times seemed to be his most creative—and what energies he had went into writing hymns, including "As with Gladness Men of Old" and "What Child Is This?" Aged only twenty-four, he published *Hymns of Love and Joy*.

In the midst of his own emotional and physical darkness, sick in bed on the day of the Epiphany, Dix recalled a dark night in a world without hope. He imagined the joy of those "men of old," the magi, as they realized who was about to be born and what it meant for humankind.

Just as they gladly followed the star, Dix wrote, so should we in these modern times. Even as they humbly bent the knee and gave of their most precious possessions, so still should we.

The carol ends with a plea to "keep us in the narrow way" until we reach the place where Christ outshines the brightest star and we can sing our alleluias to Him in person.

Almost nineteen hundred years after the birth of Christ, Dix reminded his contemporaries that the gift of a Messiah was no less wondrous than when it happened. It was a gift that shone through the centuries, shone through Dix's illness, and continues to shine today.

More than a century after William Dix's death, we have no less reason to be glad than did those "men of old"—and they were very glad indeed!

*When they had heard the king, they departed; and,*
*lo, the star, which they saw in the east, went before them,*
*till it came and stood over where the young child was.*
*When they saw the star, they rejoiced with exceeding great joy.*
Matthew 2:9–10

## As with Gladness, Men of Old

As with glad-ness, men of old    Did the guid-ing    star be-hold

As with gladness, men of old
Did the guiding star behold,
As with joy they hailed its light—
Leading onward, beaming bright,
So, most gracious Lord, may we
Evermore be led to Thee.

## Carol of the Bells

Hark! how the bells Sweet sil-ver bells   All seem to say,   "Throw cares a-w

Hark how the bells,
sweet silver bells,
all seem to say,
throw cares away.

Christmas is here,
bringing good cheer,
to young and old,
meek and the bold.

# Bountiful

"Carol of the Bells" is proof that it isn't only people who can be born again. Starting as a pagan chant, it has now become synonymous with Christmas, going through several transformations on the way.

Ukrainian music teacher and composer Mykola Leontovich took the original chant—the structure of which may have dated from prehistoric times—and used it to create the choral piece *Shchedryk*, or "Bountiful."

The lyrics initially had nothing to do with Christmas. *Shchedryk* was a New Year song in a country where the New Year was traditionally celebrated in April. It told of a swallow flying into a home and darting from room to room, excitedly telling the family of bountiful times to come.

This promise of a brighter future may have struck a popular nationalist note for Ukrainians during a short-lived period of independence from the USSR.

Premiered in 1916, *Shchedryk* was first heard in the United States in 1921 when the Ukrainian National Chorus performed at Carnegie Hall. One listener, for whom the song must have had a special resonance, was Peter Wilhousky, a Ukrainian-American choral director.

Inspired by the "pealing" tones of the vocals, Wilhousky wrote new lyrics for the tune. Focusing on images of bells and carolers, Wilhousky turned *Shchedryk* into "Carol of the Bells," a full-fledged Christmas carol.

That might seem an unusual journey for a musical piece, but it would be a familiar experience for many individuals and even cultures. For a long time, it was pagan—until a messenger came with news of freedom and the promise of better times to come. With just a little more tweaking—the sparrow with its happy news became Jesus' birth at Christmastime—it came into the fold, becoming Christian through and through.

What could be more Christmas-like than a carol redeemed and reborn?

*And she coming in that instant gave thanks likewise unto the Lord, and spake of him to all them that looked for redemption in Jerusalem.*
Luke 2:38

# "Come See the Christ Child!"

"Bring a Torch, Jeanette, Isabella," is a whimsy! It is wishful thinking—but the wish behind it has to be one of the best ever. "Ah, that we had realized on that first night who had come among us!"

Jeanette and Isabella, according to the carol, were milkmaids who found an amazing sight in their master's stables: a newborn child they knew immediately to be Jesus, the Christ. They ran out to spread the word to the rest of the village and came back bearing torches so everyone could see.

Even amid the excitement they shushed everyone, lest they disturb the child's blessed dreams.

"Bring a Torch, Jeanette, Isabella," was not originally a Christmas carol. It began life as a fourteenth-century dance tune. The French nobility liked to indulge in a lively *ritournelle*, and it was for this that the unusually upbeat tune (for a carol) was composed. The lyrics are believed to have come from either Anjou or Burgundy, and the two were first paired in print in a private publication, *Songs of the First Advent of Jesus Christ*, in 1553. Three hundred years later it crossed the sea to England and eventually became a firm favorite in America.

Back in France, in Provence, children still dress up as shepherds and milkmaids to sing the carol on their way to Christmas Eve services.

How might the story have turned out if two such wise young women *had* alerted everyone to the miracle they found in a barn? Of course, a world in which Christ was worshipped from the beginning probably would have had no need for a Savior in the first place. We know that's not real life—but we can wish and wonder all the same.

*And they came with haste, and found Mary, and Joseph,*
*and the babe lying in a manger.*
*And when they had seen it, they made known abroad the saying*
*which was told them concerning this child.*
Luke 2:16–17

Bring a Torch, Jeanette, Isabella

Bring a torch, Jean - ette, Is - a - bel - la,

Bring a torch, Jeanette, Isabella!
Bring a torch, to Bethlehem come!
Christ is born. Tell the folk of the village
Mary has laid him in a manger.
Ah! Ah! beautiful is the mother!
Ah! Ah! beautiful is her Son!

## Here We Come A-Wassailing

Here we come a - was - sail - ing  A - mong  the leaves  so  green,

Here we come a-wassailing
Among the leaves so green;
Here we come a-wandring
So fair to be seen.
Love and joy come to you,
And to you your wassail too;
And God bless you and send you
a happy New Year,
And God send you a happy New Year.

# Salute the Real Lord King

The custom of wassailing at Christmas, or midwinter, is a long and sometimes gory one! It was an old tradition among the Saxon people before they crossed the North Sea to Britain.

Sometime in the fifth century, the Saxon princess Rowena presented British king Vortigern with the skull of an enemy. The skull was full of wine, and she offered the trophy with the salutation, "Lord King, *wass-heil*!"

"Wass-heil" means "good health," and while it might not have done much for the health of the poor fellow who donated the skull, it worked wonders for Vortigern and Rowena, who married shortly afterward.

In (slightly) more civilized times, Vortigern and Rowena's descendants in the southeast of England would descend upon their fruit orchards on the twelfth night of Christmas. Fueled by home-grown cider, either they would threaten their trees with the ax if they didn't produce a good crop the following year, or they would bless them with whatever cider hadn't already been drunk.

As the tradition moved away from the countryside into the city, it was taken up by waifs and orphan children who would go from house to house singing blessings for "donations." Older carolers would take bowls of mulled wine, beer, or cider and cinnamon and sell drinks along with their blessings.

The resultant drunken revelry often got out of hand. During the Puritan period, when Christmas was canceled, many people who might have had their houses invaded by wassailers probably breathed a sigh of relief.

These days going wassailing is a happier, more loving experience. Hot drinks, alcoholic or otherwise, might be imbibed—but the event is much more about celebrating Christmas with friends, singing joyfully, and bestowing blessings.

Doing things the "traditional" way has a lot to recommend it, but when it comes to wassailing, well. . .let's stick to saluting the real "Lord King," Jesus Christ, and leave drinking from skulls and scaring fruit trees firmly in the past.

*And he took the cup, and gave thanks,*
*and gave it to them, saying,*
*Drink ye all of it.*
Matthew 26:27

# The Greater Day

It would be difficult to imagine Christmas without "Joy to the World," but there was a time when this fine old traditional hymn seemed quite revolutionary—and it isn't even about Christmas!

Isaac Watts, a Plymouth Nonconformist, was known as the father of English hymnody both for the quality of the hymns he wrote and because he led the way in penning "original songs of Christian experience." Previously, songs of worship had consisted largely of the Psalms and biblical verses set to music. Watts acknowledges Psalm 98 as his inspiration, but the words are mostly his own.

The hymn was sung for a hundred years before it found "Antioch," the tune we know it by today. The words of England's premier hymn writer inspired one of America's foremost composers of hymn music, Lowell Mason (who may also have supplied the music for another of Watts's hymns, "When I Survey the Wondrous Cross").

In 1839 Mason published the first printed collection to feature "Joy to the World" and included a note saying the music was "from Handel." By this he may have meant he "borrowed" a few sections from Handel's *Messiah*—but the public at large came to believe Handel had composed the entire piece.

"Joy to the world! the Lord is come" could easily be taken as a reference to the Nativity, but there is no manger, no Mary, no wise men.

No—Watts had in mind a greater day. His hymn is about Christ coming back to claim this world as His own. In other words, it is about the *Second* Coming, when even the hills and valleys will be purified. The land will be freed from the curse placed on it after Adam's fall from grace. People will sing and rejoice under the Lord's reign, but the celebration won't be confined to human-kind. His joy will be for the whole world—rocks and all!

*And there shall be no more curse: but the throne of God*
*and of the Lamb shall be in it; and his servants shall serve him.*
Revelation 22:3

## Joy to the World

Joy to the world, the Lord is come! Let earth re-ceive her King,

Joy to the world! the Lord is come;
Let earth receive her King.
Let every heart prepare Him room,
And heav'n and nature sing,
And heav'n and nature sing,
And heav'n, and heav'n and nature sing.

# The Virgin Mary Had a Baby Boy

The Vir-gin Ma - ry had a ba-by boy, The Vir-gin Ma - ry ha

The virgin Mary had a baby boy,
The virgin Mary had a baby boy,
The virgin Mary had a baby boy,
And they say that His name is Jesus.

# The Calypso Carol Singers

The virgin birth is a major tenet of the Christian faith, so when French and Spanish settlers sailed for the New World, they took with them this first major indicator of Christ's divinity.

Landing in the West Indies, they began to spread the word. A few of the more enlightened missionaries tapped into the rich musical traditions they found and adapted them as an effective way of teaching the gospel, which may be why "The Virgin Mary Had a Baby Boy" has a calypso lilt to it.

A very simple retelling of the Nativity, "The Virgin Mary Had a Baby Boy" relies heavily on rhythm and repetition. It can be picked up very quickly and sung by any kind of voice. Its regular beat makes it an ideal accompaniment to the monotony of a hard day's work.

From the work of those early missionaries there grew a tradition of *parang*, almost a West Indian version of carol singing. The *parrandero* would go from house to house singing praise songs, many of which they had learned working on plantations.

Edric Connor, a Trinidadian, took this song and others to London, where he carved out a career for himself as an actor and calypso singer. He put "The Virgin Mary Had a Baby Boy" into print, for possibly the first time, in 1945.

The great Harry Belafonte, sometimes known as "the king of Calypso," recorded the song in 1958 and introduced it to the American audience.

Whether being sung in a field under a hot sun or in the more organized setting of a formal choir, "The Virgin Mary Had a Baby Boy" has a distinct advantage over other songs in that it can easily be repeated with no lack of joy until everyone has had the chance to sing. Which is, after all, what the Virgin's baby boy was all about. He wasn't for an elite few—He was a gift for everyone!

*And Mary said, Behold the handmaid of the Lord;*
*be it unto me according to thy word.*
*And the angel departed from her.*
Luke 1:38

# The Gift That Keeps on Giving

John Henry Hopkins Jr. had two claims to fame: He delivered the eulogy for President Grant, and he wrote the Christmas classic "We Three Kings of Orient Are."

Posterity gave him the nickname "Vermont's Father Christmas." Needless to say, he wasn't actually Santa. He wasn't even born in Vermont. The inaccuracies carried on in the title of his famous carol.

We know from the Bible that three gifts were given to the Christ child, but nowhere does it say there were three *givers*. Those visitors to the Nativity are described as "magi," or wise men. People simply assumed they must have been kings to give such lavish gifts.

Hopkins was a Pennsylvania clergyman. In 1857 he was a busy man—an author, designer of stained glass, and illustrator, with a parish to look after as well. But he wasn't too busy for family.

Every year the Christmas holidays would be spent with relatives in Vermont. Hopkins was a favorite with his nephews and nieces, and he liked to entertain them. This year he had a special treat for them, a new song from the Gospel of Matthew. The children's delight must have encouraged him enough to include the piece in a Christmas pageant for the New York seminary.

In 1863 the song appeared in Hopkins's collection *Carols, Hymns, and Songs*. Two years later its increased fame merited a special illustrated publication of its own. Since then it has been sung around the world.

Hopkins may have been perpetuating a tradition that wasn't strictly accurate—but it really didn't matter. His song is one of worship and praise. It was a gift to the children of his family; it was a gift to the rest of us for many Christmases to come. It celebrates the gifts of gold, frankincense, and myrrh, and the greatest gift the world has ever known—a Savior!

*And when they were come into the house, they saw the young child with Mary his mother, and fell down, and worshipped him: and when they had opened their treasures, they presented unto him gifts; gold, and frankincense and myrrh.*

Matthew 2:11

We Three Kings of Orient Are

We three kings of O - ri - ent are; Bear - ing gifts we trav - erse a - far,

We three kings of Orient are;
Bearing gifts we traverse afar—
Field and fountain, moor and mountain—
Following yonder star.

O star of wonder, star of night,
Star with royal beauty bright,
Westward leading, still proceeding,
Guide us to thy perfect light.

# About the Author

DAVID MCLAUGHLAN used to write whatever turned a buck, but now he writes about faith and God. It doesn't pay as well—but it does make his heart sing! He lives in bonnie Scotland with Julie and a whole "clan" of children.